HOW BIG?

by Nicholas Harris

BLACKBIRCH™
PRESS

THOMSON
★
GALE

Detroit • New York • San Diego • San Francisco • Cleveland • New Haven, Conn. • Waterville, Maine • London • Munich

HOW TO USE THIS BOOK

For each double page, all the illustrations are drawn to scale. The biggest thing is also featured on the following double page, where it appears as the *smallest* thing. (You can find it quickly because its label is contained in a box.) The illustrations on this double page are also all drawn to scale and the biggest thing is again featured on the next double page. And so on, all the way through the book.

MEASUREMENTS

Where the metric equivalent is given, the conversion is approximate.

0.0002 inches *means* two ten-thousandths of an inch.

0.002 inches *means* two thousandths of an inch.

0.06 inches *means* six hundredths of an inch.

0.1 inches *means* one tenth of an inch.

in *is an abbreviation of* inches.

mm *is an abbreviation of* millimeter.

cm *is an abbreviation of* centimeter.

m *is an abbreviation of* meter.

km *is an abbreviation of* kilometer.

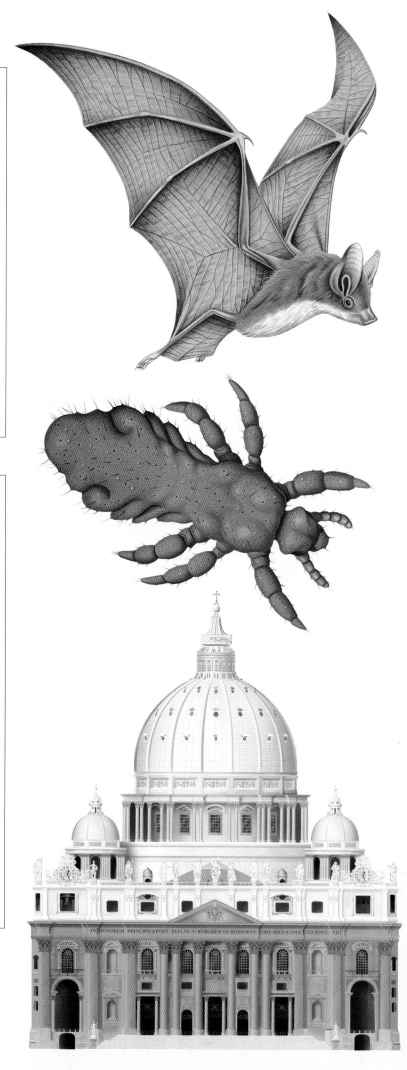

CONTENTS

YOU WOULD NEED a very powerful microscope to see the objects on this page in any detail. It would have to magnify them up to a million times!

Your body is made up of countless billions of "building blocks" called cells. Different kinds of cells make up different parts: nerve cells, skin cells, liver cells, and so on. There are two kinds of cells that make up the blood: red and white. Red blood cells carry oxygen around the body. White blood cells help protect against germs. A drop of blood the size of a pinhead contains about 9,000 white cells and 5 million red cells.

To the naked eye, pollen looks like a fine powder. Pollen is vital for a plant to be able to reproduce. It is carried by insects or other animals, or blown on the wind. Spiky pollen sticks to the furry body of an animal. Wind-borne pollen is smooth.

Each grid square on this page represents 0.001 x 0.001 inches

Crystal of table salt 0.002 in (0.05 mm)

Red blood cell 0.0002 in (0.005 mm)

White blood cell 0.0006 in (0.015 mm)

Table salt also looks like a fine powder. Seen close up, the grains have a regular, flat-sided, cubic shape. They are known as crystals. Different substances have different crystal shapes *(see pages 8-9).*

Pollen grain
0.002 in (0.05 mm)

E VERYTHING on these pages can be seen with the naked eye, but only a microscope would show details. A single snow crystal, for example, has a six-rayed star shape. A computer microchip, which controls the way a computer operates, is a maze of electronic circuits and parts.

Each grid square on this page represents 0.04 x 0.04 inches

Pollen grain 0.002 in (0.05 mm)

Grains of sand 0.02 in (0.5 mm) on average

8

Grains of sand from a beach or desert dunes have smooth surfaces because they have been rubbed together by the sea or by the wind.

A head louse lives by sucking blood from its host—people. It uses its massive claws to grip strands of hair so tightly that it is not easily shaken off!

The yellow meadow ant lives in nests of thousands of ants. It feeds on honeydew, the waste from tinier insects called aphids.

Computer microchip 0.04 in (1 mm)

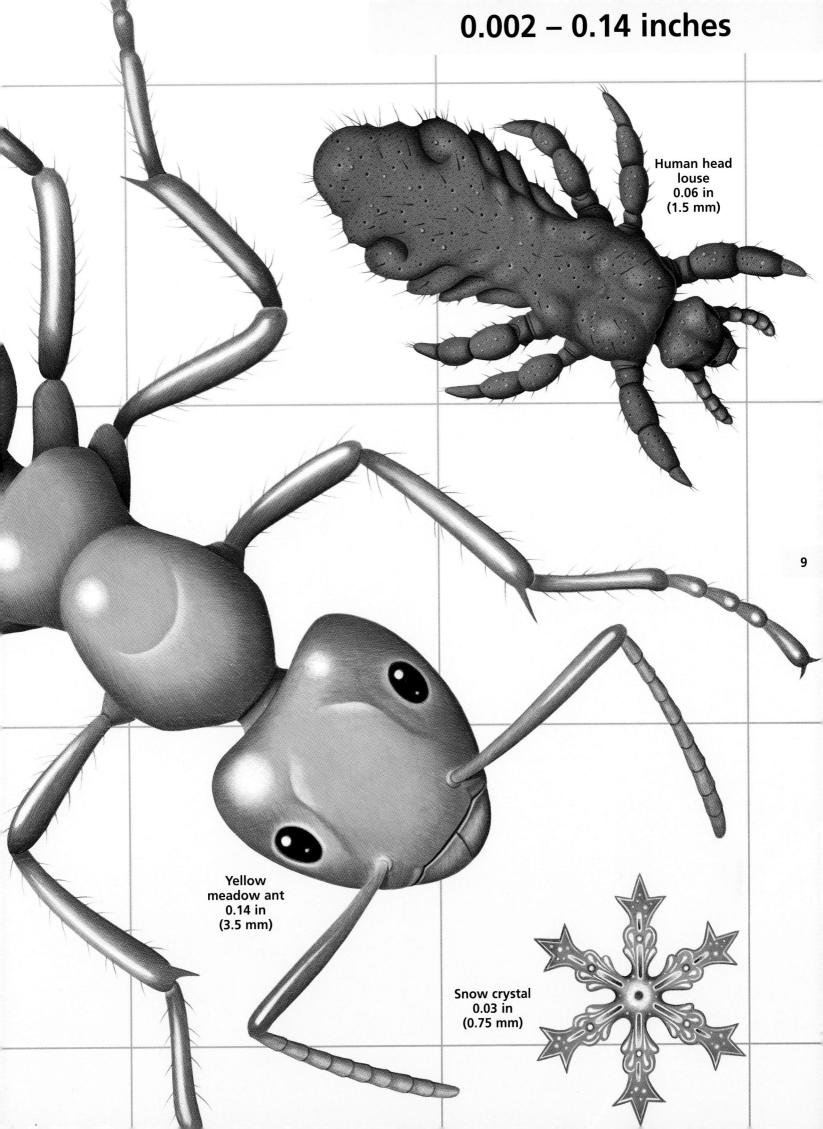

0.002 – 0.14 inches

Human head
louse
0.06 in
(1.5 mm)

9

Yellow
meadow ant
0.14 in
(3.5 mm)

Snow crystal
0.03 in
(0.75 mm)

INSECTS come in an incredibly wide range of sizes. Some are so tiny you can only see them through a microscope. Others are larger than some mammals. The rhinoceros beetle is many times bigger and heavier than the yellow meadow ant. When fighting, the male uses its horns to lift a rival male out of the way. In fact, it can lift 850 times its own weight!

Butterflies must be light enough to fly. Some tropical kinds are very large, with wingspans of 10 inches (25 cm) or more. The monarch butterfly is famous for the incredible journey it makes. It flies from the northern USA, to the forests of Mexico where it spends winter—a distance of 1,800 miles (3,000 km).

A mouse is a familiar small animal, but the Kitti's hog-nosed bat is even smaller. Little larger than a bumblebee, it is the world's smallest bat. Its wingspan is just 6 inches (15 cm). This tiny bat has a large appetite. It eats up to four times its own weight in insects every day.

Each grid square on this page represents 1.5 x 1.5 inches

House mouse
2.5 in (6.5 cm body length
tail 2.4 in (6 cm)

Yellow meadow ant
0.14 in (3.5 mm)

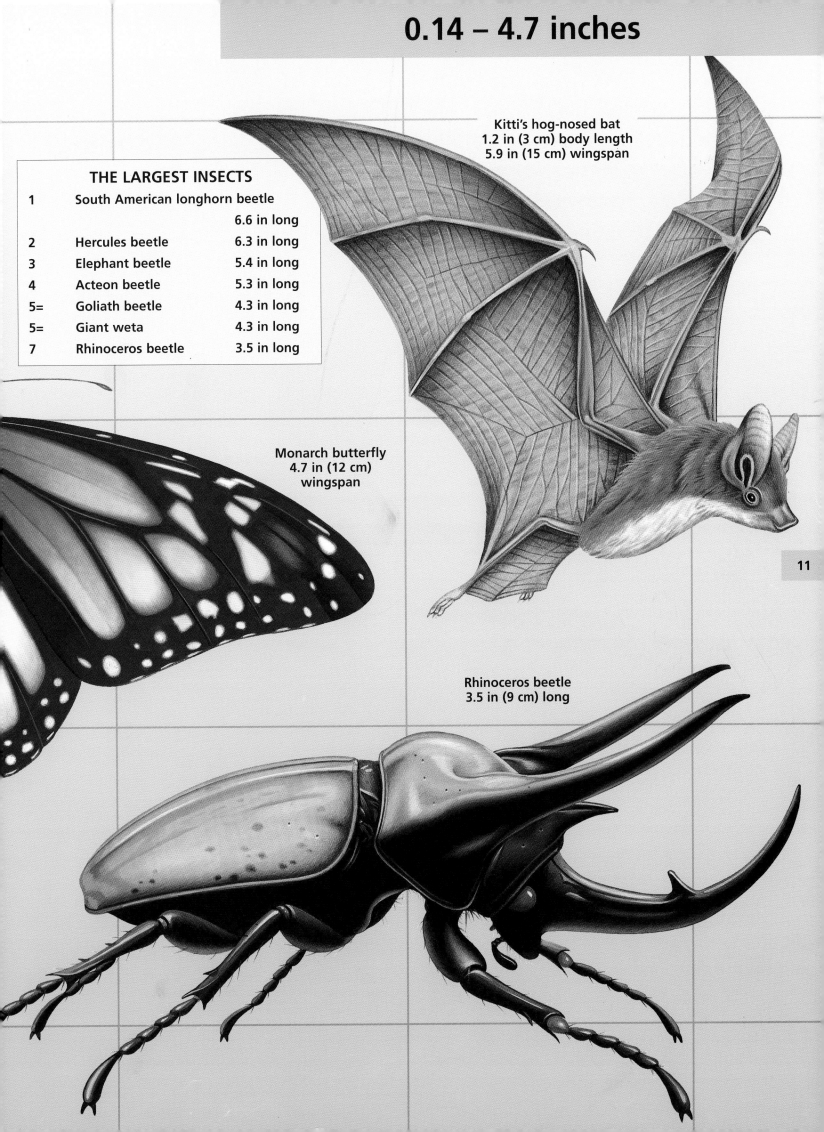

Kitti's hog-nosed bat
1.2 in (3 cm) body length
5.9 in (15 cm) wingspan

THE LARGEST INSECTS

1	South American longhorn beetle	
		6.6 in long
2	Hercules beetle	6.3 in long
3	Elephant beetle	5.4 in long
4	Acteon beetle	5.3 in long
5=	Goliath beetle	4.3 in long
5=	Giant weta	4.3 in long
7	Rhinoceros beetle	3.5 in long

Monarch butterfly
4.7 in (12 cm)
wingspan

11

Rhinoceros beetle
3.5 in (9 cm) long

BIRDS come in a wide range of sizes. The largest bird, the ostrich, can grow to about 8 feet (2.4 m) and weigh 300 pounds (135 kg). The smallest bird, the bee hummingbird, is only 2.5 inches (6.5 cm) long and weighs just 0.1 ounces (2.5 g). One of the largest flying birds, the wandering albatross, weighs 20 pounds (9 kg). Its wingspan of 11.5 feet (3.5 m) is the longest of any bird. Using the strong ocean winds, it often glides and soars for days at a time. It watches out for fish and squid in the waters below.

The magpie is a tough, intelligent, and adaptable bird. A strong flier, it feeds on anything it can find, including insects, snails, small mammals, carrion, fruit— and even other birds.

Magpie
20 in (50 cm) long

12

Each grid square on
this page represents
10 x 10 inches

Domestic cat
20 in (50 cm) long
excluding tail

Monarch butterfly
4.7 in (12 cm)
wingspan

THE LARGEST BIRDS

Tallest and heaviest bird ostrich	8 ft /300 lb
Tallest ever bird New Zealand giant moa	12 ft
Heaviest ever bird Dromornis stitorni	1,000 lb
Tallest flying birds crane family	6.6 ft
Heaviest flying bird Kori bustard	46 lb
Heaviest bird of prey Andean condor	22 lb
Heaviest sea bird Northern royal albatross	19 lb
Largest wingspan wandering albatross	11.5 ft
Largest wingspan of land bird marabou stork	10.5 ft
Longest bill Australian pelican	18.5 in

Wandering albatross
4.4 ft (135 cm) long

Six-month-old
baby
28 in (70 cm) tall

13

ELEPHANTS are the largest land-living animals. There are two kinds: the African and Asian elephant. An African elephant has the larger ears. It has two fingerlike extensions on the end of its trunk, while the Asian elephant has only one.

The African elephant is also the larger of the two. It eats 440 pounds (200 kg) of vegetation each day, using its trunk to grasp leaves, shoots, and twigs.

The horned dinosaur, *Triceratops*, was another massive planteater, but it lived 65 million years ago. An average-sized *Triceratops* might have weighed about 10 tons Neither animal, however, would be a match for a dump truck, which weighs about 20 tons.

African elephant
10.8 ft (3.3 m) tall
at the shoulder

Wandering albatross
4.4 ft (135 cm) long

THE HEAVIEST ANIMALS
(excluding whales)

1	African elephant	7 tons
2=	White rhinoceros	3.6 tons
2=	Elephant seal	3.6 tons
4	Hippopotamus	2.5–4 tons
5	Giraffe	1.6 tons
6	Walrus	1.2 tons
7	Steller sea lion	1.1 tons
8=	American bison	1 ton
8=	Polar bear	1 ton
10	Buffalo	1,210–1,870 pounds

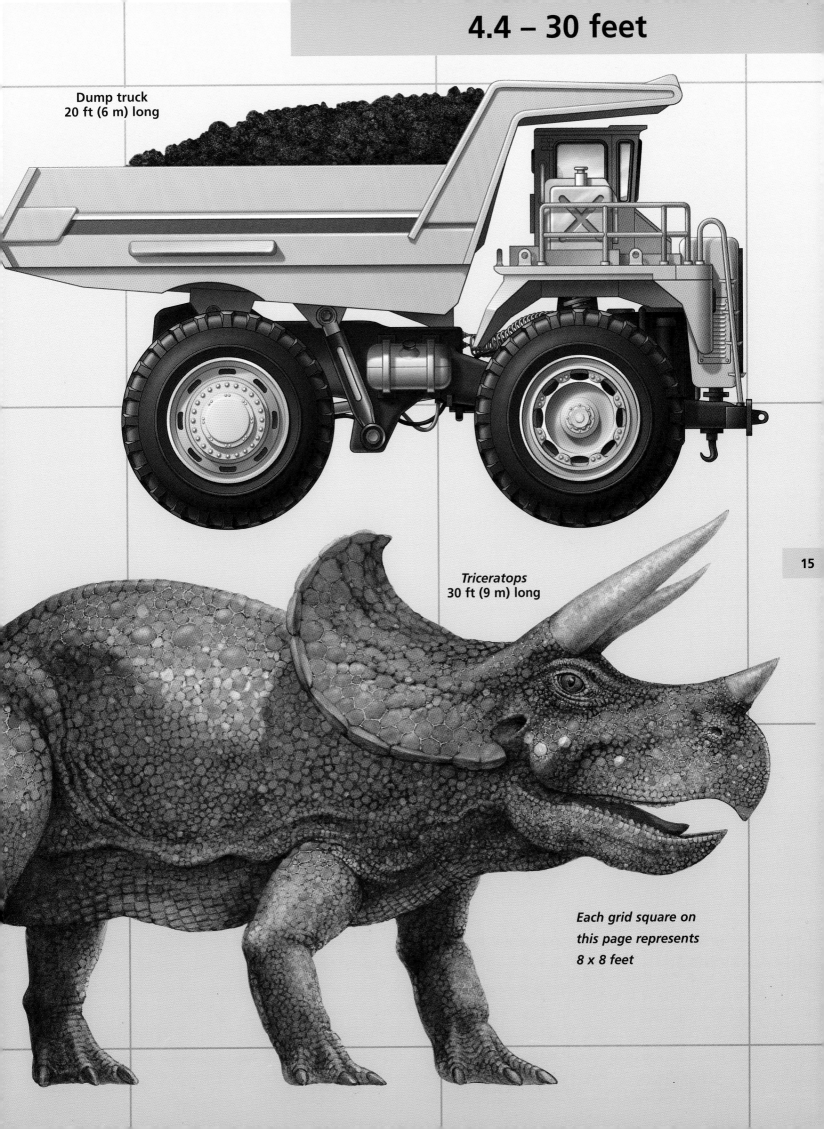

4.4 – 30 feet

Dump truck
20 ft (6 m) long

Triceratops
30 ft (9 m) long

15

*Each grid square on
this page represents
8 x 8 feet*

ANY LARGE ANIMAL, living or extinct, would look tiny on this page—even compared to a large tree. A giant sequoia tree, known as "General Sherman," is the most massive living thing. It is more than 3,000 years old and, at over 2,000 tons, is 13 times the weight of a blue whale.

One of the greatest structures ever made by humans is also one of the oldest standing. The Great Pyramid of Khufu at Giza, Egypt, was built in about 2580 B.C. It was built using 2.3 million blocks of limestone. Each weighed on average about 2.5 tons. The pyramid may have taken 30 years to build. Its base is almost a perfect square. Each face points exactly north, south, east, and west. It was the world's tallest structure for 4,000 years.

St Peter's, Vatican City, was the world's largest church for nearly 400 years. Begun in 1507, it took more than 150 years to complete. It has since lost its record to the Church of Our Lady of Peace in Yamoussoukro, Ivory Coast.

Great Pyramid
482 ft (147 m) tall
754 ft (230 m) across

St Peter's
460 ft (140 m) tall
695 ft (212 m) long

Each grid square
on this page
represents
200 x 200 ft

Grand Princess
cruise liner
950 ft (290 m) long

INHONOREM PRINCIPIS·APOST PAVLVS·V·BVRGHESIVS·ROMANVS PONT·MAX·ANMD

Triceratops
30 ft (9 m) long

Of all forms of transport, only ships can be compared in size with the greatest buildings. The *Grand Princess*, launched in 1998, can carry 2,600 passengers. Its 18 decks include several swimming pools, a theater, and a wedding chapel.

The Lockheed C-5A, which first flew in 1968, is one of the largest aircraft ever built. With four massive jet engines, it can easily carry two tanks and 16 trucks.

THE LARGEST SHIPS

		gross tonnage	length
1	*Jahre Viking*	260,851	1,505 ft
2	*Eagle* class	136,000	1,020 ft
3	*Grand Princess*	109,000	950 ft
4	*Carnival Destiny*	101,353	892 ft
5	USS *Nimitz*	98,500	1,092 ft
6	*Mediterranean*	95,000	987 ft
7	*Queen Elizabeth 1*	83,673	1,030 ft
8	*Normandie*	82,799	1,027 ft
9	*Queen Mary*	81,235	1,020 ft
10	*Norway*	76,049	1,036 ft

Ushiku Amida Buddha
(world's largest statue)
394 ft (120 m) tall
4,000 tons

Lockheed C-5A
transporter plane
246 ft (75 m) long
223 ft (68 m)
wingspan

17

"General Sherman"
giant sequoia
275 ft (84 m) tall
36 ft (11 m) across

THE GREAT PYRAMID is a colossal structure, but it is tiny when compared to the giants of nature. For example, the Grand Canyon in Arizona or Uluru (Ayers Rock) in Australia, are both much bigger than anything built by people.

The Devil's Tower in Wyoming is a natural, flat-topped "pyramid." It was once a volcano, but its outer layers were quickly stripped away by erosion, leaving behind a core of solid magma.

Each grid square on this page represents 4,000 x 4,000 ft

18

Grand Canyon
1 mile (1,600 m) average depth
10 miles (16 km) average width
217 miles (349 km) long

Devil's Tower
height above plain 1,280 ft (390 m)
276 ft (84 m) across summit
1,000 ft (305 m) across base

Great Pyramid
482 ft (147 m) tall
754 ft (230 m) across

**Mount Fuji
12,385 ft (3776 m) high**

A much larger volcano, Mount St. Helens, in Washington State, erupted in 1980. During that eruption, 141,000 cubic feet (4 cubic kilometers) of volcanic ash were blasted out into the sky. More than 1,300 feet (400 m) of the mountain's original height was lost. The perfect cone of Mount Fuji, Japan, has, by contrast, remained unchanged since it last erupted in 1707.

**Mount St Helens
present height 8,364 ft (2,550 m)
height before eruption 9,676 ft (2,950 m)**

**Uluru (Ayers Rock)
1,141 ft (348 m) high
1.9 miles (3.1 km) long**

THE PLANET MARS is orbited by two potato-shaped moons, Deimos and Phobos. Both are made of bare, dark rock. Deimos has fewer craters than Phobos. There is a crater measuring 6 miles (10 km) across on Phobos called Stickney.

Both moons were probably once asteroids, rocky bodies of different sizes that orbit the Sun (mostly between Mars and Jupiter) in their millions. Some time ago, they started to orbit Mars. Phobos orbits Mars just 3,714 miles (5,980 km) above its surface. Astronomers think it will eventually crash onto the Martian surface—in about 50 million years time!

Each grid square on this page represents 3 x 3 miles

Deimos 10 miles (16 km) across

12,385 feet – 17 miles

Phobos
17 miles (28 km)
across

Mount Fuji
12,385 ft (3,776 m) high

THE MOON is a ball of rock that travels around Earth. All the other planets apart from Mercury and Venus have moons. Most are tiny when compared in size with their parent planet. Our Moon, on the other hand, is more than a quarter the size of Earth. Its barren landscape is peppered with craters. They have been blasted out by rocks from space, called meteorites, crashing to the Moon's surface.

One of Uranus's 21 moons, Miranda, is much smaller than Earth's moon. Its surface is a jumble of cliffs, canyons, and craters. There is also a V-shaped zone of "grooves."

Pluto is the smallest, coldest, and outermost planet in the solar system. Its surface is probably made of ice—not water ice, but a mixture of frozen nitrogen, carbon monoxide, and methane.

22

**Phobos
17 miles (28 km)
across**

**Miranda
292 miles
(470 km)
across**

Moon
2,159 miles
(3,476 km) across

THE LARGEST MOONS

		parent planet	*diameter*
1	Ganymede	Jupiter	3,272 miles
2	Titan	Saturn	3,199 miles
3	Callisto	Jupiter	2,985 miles
4	Io	Jupiter	2,265 miles
5	Moon	Earth	2,159 miles
6	Europa	Jupiter	1,944 miles
7	Triton	Neptune	1,680 miles
8	Titania	Uranus	980 miles
9	Rhea	Saturn	949 miles
10	Oberon	Uranus	946 miles

Pluto
1,443 miles
(2,324 km)
across

ERCURY is the second-smallest planet in the solar system and the closest to the Sun. It has the greatest extremes of temperature. During the day it can be more than 700°F (400°C), The night-time temperature falls to –300°F(–170°C).

Mars, the third-smallest planet, is named the Red Planet for the rusty colored dust that blankets it. Evidence exists that there was once running water on Mars. (The only water there now is frozen.) So it is possible that life could once have existed on the Red Planet.

Each grid square on this page represents 3,000 x 3,000 miles

Mars
4,220 miles
(6,794 km)
across

Moon
2,159 miles
(3,476 km)
across

Mercury
3,030 miles
(4,878 km)
across

Venus
7,518 miles
(12,104 km)
across

Venus and Earth are almost exactly the same size, but they are not similar in any other way. Venus is covered by thick clouds of deadly sulfuric acid. The air is unbreathable carbon dioxide. Its surface temperature is a constant 880°F (490°C)—hotter than the melting point of lead.

THE PLANETS IN ORDER OF SIZE
diameter

1	Jupiter	88,803 miles
2	Saturn	74,867 miles
3	Uranus	31,770 miles
4	Neptune	31,390 miles
5	Earth	7,923 miles
6	Venus	7,518 miles
7	Mars	4,220 miles
8	Mercury	3,030 miles
9	Pluto	1,443 miles

Earth
7,923 miles
(12,756 km) across

25

K NOWN as the "gas giants", Jupiter, Saturn, Uranus, and Neptune are the largest planets in the Solar System. They each have thick, gassy outer layers with no solid surfaces at all. Jupiter, the largest, is more massive than all the other planets combined—including its fellow gas giants. It could contain more than 1,300 Earths.

Uranus
31,770 miles
(51,118 km)
across

Neptune
31,390 miles
(50,538 km)
across

Earth
7,923 miles
(12,756 km) across

Although it is the second-largest planet, Saturn is the least dense of them all. If a large enough bathtub of water could be found, Saturn would float in it! Saturn's quick rotation causes it to bulge at its equator. Its wide rings are made up of billions of blocks of ice and rock.

Uranus and Neptune both have very faint ring systems. Their featureless, gassy surfaces are sometimes flecked by clouds traveling at high speeds.

Each grid square on this page represents 30,000 x 30,000 miles

Saturn
74,867 miles
(120,536 km) across
excluding rings

Jupiter
88,803 miles
(142,884 km)
across

THE SUN is the biggest object in the Solar System. In fact, it contains more than 99% of all matter in the Solar System. Its diameter is 10 times that of Jupiter, and more than 100 times that of Earth. Yet the Sun is really only an ordinary star. Compared to other stars, it is actually below average size.

Like all stars, the Sun is a spinning ball of extremely hot gas. Made mostly of hydrogen and helium gases, it creates huge amounts of energy by fusing hundreds of millions of tons of hydrogen every second. Without the Sun's warming rays, no life at all could exist on Earth.

The temperature of the Sun's outer shell is 11,000°F (5500°C). It is about 27 million°F (15 million°C) at its core. The surface is constantly bubbling, like water in a kettle. Occasionally, huge arches of fire, called prominences, or explosions of energy, called flares, burst out. Darker, cooler areas, known as sunspots, appear on the Sun's surface from time to time.

Jupiter
88,900 miles
(142,984 km)
across

Sun
869,565 miles
(1,400,000 km)
across